THE LANDSCAPES of KENT

ROD COOPER

– Photographs by –

DAVID SELLMAN

COUNTRYSIDE BOOKS
NEWBURY, BERKSHIRE

First published 2002

Reprinted 2007

Countryside Books
3 Catherine Road
Newbury, Berkshire

To view our complete range of books,
please visit us at
www. countrysidebooks.co.uk

ISBN 1 85306 756 3
EAN 9781853 0675 63

Produced through MRM Associates Ltd., Reading
Printed in China

CONTENTS

Aylesford

FOREWORD

But as for ortchards of aples, and gardeins of cheries, and those of the most delicious and exquisite kindes that can be, no part of the realme (that I know) hath them, either in such quantitie and number, or with such arte and industrie, set and planted.

William Lambarde, 1570, *Perambulation of Kent*

Today, those fruits and the ales with the tang of Kentish hops fight off keen competition from the other side of the Channel Tunnel, and if high speed road and rail links have changed the nature of a journey through Kent, Lambarde would be happy to find how much of the county has retained its nature. Indeed, the fruits he so much admired, established in England's first large-scale orchards at Teynham by Henry VIII's fruiterer Richard Harris, still flourish just a few miles away at Brogdale, home to the National Fruit Collections. This comprises the largest collection of varieties of fruit trees and plants in the world, including literally thousands of different kinds of apple, and many hundreds, more of pear, plum, cherry and bush fruits.

Throughout the county there is still a great abundance of orchards and hop gardens, hedgerows and coppices, with oast houses and barns, restored and adapted for domestic living, but retaining a beauty of their own. Nearly 90 per cent of land in the county is still rural. Large tracts of it have that distinctive Kentish character, and the market towns and villages at its heart could certainly belong in no other county. The Northern Downs and the wooded High Weald are as beautiful as ever and the marshlands of the Thames Estuary and Romney Marsh retain much of their mystery. The great houses and castles, the handsome parish churches and the famous gardens are now enjoyed by a cosmopolitan public. Tourists and hikers have replaced pilgrims on the ancient pathways.

Kent has never regretted its close proximity to London on the one hand and to the Continent on the other, for that has always determined its way of life, keeping the capital city supplied with anything from cherries to bricks, and dispatching people and goods to foreign parts. Much of its beauty is born of such practical purposes. Kent has had to earn its living. The beautiful photographs in this book capture the nature of this unique county vividly and show just why we must never take our familiar, much-loved landscapes for granted.

The White Cliffs

... that pale, that white faced shore,
Whose foot spurns back the ocean's roaring tides

William Shakespeare, *King John*

For centuries the great white cliffs of Dover, built up over many millions of years, have offered the first distant sight of Britain to those, hostile or friendly, who approach by sea, the apparently unbroken line gradually dividing into the mighty Shakespeare Cliff to port and the East Cliff, crowned by the magnificent Norman castle, to starboard.

Between the two cliffs lie the Eastern and Western Docks, servicing a steady succession of ferries and other ships, despite the opening of the Channel Tunnel, which has made its own contribution to Dover's white landscape. At the foot of the Shakespeare Cliff, accessible by a tunnel through the cliffs reached from the Dover to Folkestone road, is Samphire Hoe, made from millions of tons of chalk dug out to create the Channel Tunnel and offering wild flowers including orchids, birds, butterflies, sea angling, walks, and peaceful spots for picnics.

The harbour has always been at the heart of the town's history. Julius Caesar found that these cliffs offered too much protection to the fierce defenders when he came here in 55 BC and he hastily sought a quieter landing place near Deal. The castle offers stunning views from the top of the keep, as do the white clifftop paths of Dover, running north to protect St Margaret's Bay and south to Folkestone. Let Shakespeare have the last word, too, on the cliff that bears his name. In *King Lear*, Edgar takes his poor blind father, Gloucester, to this lofty 'chalky bourne' from where:

Dover Harbour has always been at the heart of the town's history

The crows and choughs that wing the midway air
Show scarce so gross as beetles; half way down
Hangs one that gathers samphire, dreadful trade;
Methinks he seems no bigger than his head.
The fishermen that walk upon the beach
Appear like mice ... The murmuring surge
That on th'unnumbered idle pebbles chafes
Cannot be heard so high ...

St Margaret's Bay, where Channel swimmers start and finish their epic personal battles

The First Fields of England

Green fields of England! whereso'er
Across this watery waste we fare,
Your image at our hearts we bear,
Green fields of England, everywhere!

Arthur Hugh Clough, *Green Fields of England!*

Behind the coast road between Dover and Folkestone lies the Alkham Valley. The landscape here ripples and swells like another sea, with waves of downland and woods forever offering a fresh surprise in the next deep hollow or over a sudden crest as the shadows of clouds chase each other across the countryside.

This is a valley of little lanes, woods, and meadows. Alkham itself lies snugly sheltered on a crossroads in a deep depression, although it has quite the opposite effect on the spirits. The village is a cluster of handsome houses and cottages with terraced gardens, nestling near the fine old flint, square-towered church rebuilt by the monks of St Radegund's abbey in the 13th century. The north aisle was soon replaced by a chapel with wonderful mural arcading. A short walk away stand the abbey ruins, an ivy-covered gatehouse which was once the tower, and a 16th-century farmhouse, formerly the refectory.

One of the best ways to enjoy this lovely valley is on horseback. The Alkham Valley Rides provide 20 miles of spectacular scenic riding on the North Downs to both sides of the valley. The route is well waymarked with blue arrows inside black horseshoes. For the walker, any lane will do: find the footpath if you can from the abbey to Copt Hill, or walk the long lane to Wootton with its little 13th-century church. And if the walks end in despair in the corner of a cornfield, as they have a habit of doing in this valley, the serene beauty of the surroundings soon calms the frustrations; and there are always sudden surprises, like a brief glimpse of a distant Dover Castle through the heat haze.

The village of Alkham

In the Alkham Valley

IN DEFENCE OF KENT'S COASTLINE

I hear the waves dash and the tackle strain,
The canvas flap, the rattle of the chain
That runs out thro' the hawse, the clank of the winch
Winding the rusty cable inch by inch ...

Robert Southey on his childhood memories of Walmer
The Summer House on the Mound

Deal and Walmer castles, built by Henry VIII in 1540 as a precaution against invasion, are separated by a short stretch of coastline as flat and undeviating as Deal's postwar pier. The beach path between them has seen many millions of brisk and breezy constitutionals past the lifeboat station before and after lunch. A third fortress to the north at Sandown is in ruins.

Walmer Castle, base for many a Lord Warden

The castles look out across the anchorage of the Downs opposite the Goodwin Sands. Deal's is the finer, built on a concentric plan with huge curved bastions mounted with cannon and set with 52 port-holes. There is a large round tower in the centre. The walls are 20 ft thick at the foundation and reduce to about 10 ft at the top. There are spartan living quarters on the first floor, a magazine in the basement, and a drawbridge on the land side. The whole structure would have been an intimidating prospect for any invaders landing from the sea.

But Deal itself is a friendly town, with a happy marriage of brick and weather-boarded, 18th and 19th-century houses. Other familiar sights include the Time Ball Tower, which gave the time to shipping riding at anchor offshore, and the fishing boats drawn up on the shore, the only hint of danger coming from the sinister, protruding masts of a cargo ship, victim of the treacherous Goodwin Sands like so many before her.

There are fishing vessels on the beach at Walmer, too, but the castle is a less rugged affair, having been converted, with additions, into living quarters for the Lord Wardens of the Cinque Ports, most notably Lord Wellington. The room where he died has been left much as it was, austere, but oddly moving. Lady Hester Stanhope, niece of another Lord Warden, William Pitt the Younger laid out the gardens, which, like Walmer itself, are quietly pleasing.

Deal Castle, built on a concentric plan

ANCIENT AND MODERN

The sparroe hath found a house and the swallow a nest for herself.

Inscription over the doorway of Robin's Croft, one of the finest houses in Chilham.

Ashford's handsome virtues may be confined to its great parish church and some fine houses in the square around it and in the old town centre, but its importance as a road and rail centre has been enhanced by the International station on the Eurostar line. There is much recent development and modern roads strike out in all directions, but, also, for the more leisurely traveller it is a good centre for visiting some of the loveliest villages in Kent.

Chilham is a typical example. It has a wonderful square with timber-framed houses on two sides, the castle gatehouse on the third side, and the largely 15th-century church, guarded by the White Horse inn, on the fourth. This square becomes a packed car park from spring through to autumn, but the beauty of so many of the houses and the loving care with which they are tended still makes a visit very worthwhile out of season.

There have been forts here in distant times but Chilham's castle was actually a manor house built for Sir Dudley Digges in 1616. It remains a private home, standing in a magnificent park with stunning views across the Stour Valley, every bit as memorable as the falconry and jousting displays which have also brought visitors to the village.

A long barrow across the Stour, to the south of Chilham, is said to be the resting place of Julius Laberius, one of Julius Caesar's Tribunes. Known as 'Julliberrie's Grave', it is also said to mark the spot where the Britons fought a battle against the Tenth Legion in 54 BC. Any visitor persistent enough to track it down deserves refreshment back in the village. In tea shop and pub the accents of modern Rome mingle with many others. The houses have seen it all before, as have Robin's Croft's sparrows and swallows.

Ashford is at its best away from the modern office blocks

Chilham square is seen at its best out of season

Rising to the Sky

Tanta majestate sese erigit in coelum.
With what majesty it rises to the sky.

Erasmus on first seeing Canterbury Cathedral in 1513.

The Cathedral Church of Christ, Canterbury, mother church of the Anglican Communion, looks out over the roofs of the city in all its splendour. You can gaze down upon it in wonder from the hills around. There is a fine view from the campus of the University of Kent, which impresses prospective students on open days almost as much as it did Chaucer's first pilgrims when they fell to their knees and prayed at their first glimpse.

There have been many changes since Chaucer's time, and before that, too. Here stood a church consecrated in St Augustine's day, and later a Saxon cathedral, demolished in 1070 by William the Conqueror's archbishop, Lanfranc, who set about rebuilding the cathedral. His work was built on in turn by his successor, Anselm.

Those perpendicular towers on the western front are not the twins they seem from afar, the south-west one dates from the 15th century, the other is a replica which replaced Lanfranc's north-western tower as late as 1832. Some purists may not agree, but from this range the three towers work wonderfully well, the great central Bell Harry tower tying the whole form together.

You must draw far closer to appreciate the wonders of the eastern end and the work of William of Sens and William the Englishman, who built the Trinity Chapel for Becket's tomb and the remarkable Corona of Becket's Crown. And, of course, you should enter the cathedral to see the soaring nave, the great arch strengthening the supports for Bell Harry, the carving of the pillars in the Choir, the tombs of the Black Prince and of archbishops and kings, the finest stained glass in England and the constant, dramatic rise from west to east as you progress. The greatest glories are inside, but the first sight is never forgotten.

Floodlit by night

Canterbury Cathedral from the hills

AND STILL THEY COME

And specially from every shires ende
Of engelond to caunterbury they wende,
The hooly blisful martir for to seke
That hem hath holpen whan that they were sicke.

Geoffrey Chaucer
Prologue, The Canterbury Tales

From the Buttermarket, the splendid Christ Church Gate, built at the beginning of the 16th century between the city and the cathedral precincts, offers a sudden, stunning view of the vastness of the cathedral within. There was a covered market building in this small, cobblestoned square in the 17th century and two centuries later another handsome roof protected market stalls in the central area from the elements.

Today, it is constantly thronged with tourists, pausing for a rest and a drink while they listen to buskers; but then it has long been a place for enjoying liquid refreshment. Shops may occupy the sites of such 15th-century inns as The Sun and The Bull, but at every turn there are double-jettied houses that once offered sustenance to pilgrims to the shrine of St Thomas à Becket, who was murdered in his cathedral and canonized just three years later. Running into the square is the wondrously surviving medieval Mercery Lane, on one corner of which is the eastern half of The Chequer of Hope, a courtyard inn built by the cathedral priory in the 14th century which once ran back to the Buttermarket.

That steady trail of pilgrims to the shrine brought the city its wealth and prestige. The tourists of today still come to pay respects of a sort, bustling in the streets from spring through to autumn. There is so much to see in such a confined space, with the short, pedestrianised main street becoming in turn St George's Street, The Parade, High Street, Eastbridge and St Peter's Street on its way to the West Gate, each stretch with its own buildings of rare interest, and with intersecting streets offering yet more diversions.

Thomas Fyndon, Abbot of St Augustine's from 1283 to 1309, built this gateway, pictured from Lady Wootton's Garden. Charles I and Henrietta Marie spent their wedding night in the chamber above.

The Buttermarket and Christ Church Gate

SAILING AND SMUGGLING

. . . and, now and then, a little sailing boat either departed with a gay and talkative cargo of passengers, or returned with a very silent and particularly uncomfortable-looking one.

Charles Dickens on Ramsgate, *Sketches by Boz.*

Ramsgate boasts a large outer Royal Harbour where fishing and other commercial vessels bob in still lively water, and visiting craft settle at their overnight pontoons; but through the lock in the peaceful inner harbour a vast array of sailing and pleasure boats lies at berth in the still water.

Ramsgate harbour was originally built for craft seeking refuge from stormy weather. A small fishing village up to the 18th century, it gradually achieved some status as a commercial port with trade between London, Newcastle and Holland. In 1821 the people of the town gave King George IV such a loyal welcome when he voyaged to and from Hanover that he gave Ramsgate Harbour its regal title. There is an obelisk to mark his passage.

The long east and west piers make it a particularly delightful place to wander, with a host of vantage points from which to see cargoes being unloaded and fishermen and yachtsmen preparing for sea. The development of the modern marina has added to the pleasures of people and craft watching, particularly when the harbour is hosting one of the nautical festivals and events that take place here throughout the year. The Regency and Victorian prosperity is still reflected in the handsome, elegant squares and colonnaded crescents of the houses and hotels of the old resort town that run down to the harbour.

Just along the Thanet coast at Kingsgate, near Margate, the infamous Callis Court gang of smugglers fought the Revenue men in a pitched battle by these cliffs, just below the Captain Digby pub at Kingsgate, in March 1769. The smugglers were ambushed while unloading their contraband near caves which led from the shore up to the 18th-century flint inn. Farmers cut seagates, paths through the soft chalk, to carry up seaweed for the land and flints for building walls. Today, oyster catchers and ringed plover scuttle about on the shore line and fulmars nest in the stark cliffs. Wilfowl stop over in the winter and in the summer butterflies are attracted by the colourful and scented chalk-loving plants above the shore.

The cliffs at Kingsgate

Ramsgate harbour – ideal for the pleasures of people and craft watching

DICKENSIAN DELIGHTS AT THE SEASIDE

The sands are the children's great resort. They cluster there, like ants: so busy burying their particular friends, and making castles with infinite labour which the next tide overthrows ...

Charles Dickens, *Our English Watering-place*

Dickens delighted in Broadstairs, whose praises he sang constantly in letters to friends while completing *David Copperfield* and *Barnaby Rudge* here. For nine days every June at the Broadstairs Dickens Festival, visitors can enjoy scores of events related to the great man. The crinolined ladies, their top-hatted escorts and a host of favourite figures from the novels can be admired, or enthusiasts can enter into the spirit by dressing in costumes of the years in which Dickens stayed here (from 1837 to 1859) and joining them as they promenade in Dickensian splendour through the town.

Dickens familiars in front of Bleak House

He would still enjoy much of Broadstairs today for, blessed with seven sandy beaches and sheltered bays, it has been able to resist the pressures of modern life more firmly than its neighbours along the Thanet coast. Viking Bay, with its picturesque harbour, crescent shaped beach and tidal paddling pool, is still particularly enjoyed at weekends by the people of East Kent as well as by holidaymakers from farther afield.

A visit is full of nostalgia for those who remember Broadstairs immediately after the last war, when Uncle Mack and his now politically incorrect, but in those more innocent days much-loved, black and white minstrels played on the pier and on the beach, when the Band of the Royal Marines (Chatham Division) struck up *A Life on the Ocean Waves* twice daily in the promenade bandstand, and children raised on wartime rations suddenly found themselves splashing out half-a-crown on a spectacular Knickerbocker Glory, or even a five-shilling Big Boy, in one of the town's splendid Italian ice-cream parlours.

As Mr Pooter observed blissfully in a holiday entry in his *Diary of a Nobody*, 'Hurrah! at Broadstairs'. Hurrah indeed.

Broadstairs sands – 'the children's great resort'

THE TWIN SISTERS STILL KEEP WATCH

And down came the church, and what wos his thoats about his flock that day no one knows.

Parish clerk's note on the destruction of the church at Reculver, 1809.

The Romans built a fort at Reculver (Regulbium) between Herne Bay and Birchington in the third century to guard the northern entrance to the Wantsum Channel, which cut the Isle of Thanet off from the rest of Kent. In 669 AD King Egbert of Kent built within the walls a church and monastery that became an important Christian site in Saxon England. The two great towers were added in Norman times and eventually became an invaluable guide to shipping. In the 15th century the Abbess of Faversham and a sister were shipwrecked while on a pilgrimage along this stretch of the coast. The sister never recovered and in her memory the Abbess added spires to the towers, which then became known as the Twin Sisters.

By 1809 the site was becoming so badly eroded that the vicar decided to dismantle the church and move it inland. The spires had gone, but Trinity House saved the two towers for their value as a landmark to shipping and shored up the cliffs and site.

This is a caravan and chalet coastline, with the stretch on towards Herne Bay now the Reculver Country Park. Beyond Herne Bay the clifftop walker eventually comes to the grassy Tankerton Slopes and goes on past beach huts and innumerable small sailing boats down into Whitstable. In places the town still retains plenty of its character with fishermen's cottages in the Walls, between the High Street and the sea, even if the famous native oysters have largely had to give way to the farmed Pacific variety. On the waterfront the air is all fish and salt and the rattle of rigging and the harbour is a bustling commercial one.

In Whitstable Harbour

The Twin Towers of Reculver

HISTORY IS ALIVE IN FAVERSHAM

I fear me he was murdered in this house
And look about this chamber where we are
And you shall find part of his guiltless blood;
For in his slipshoe did I find some rushes,
Which argue he was murdered in this room.

Anon. *Arden of Faversham.*

In the 17th century Faversham was visited by several leading companies of players, including the one in which Shakespeare acted, and to this day the bloodthirsty Elizabethan melodrama *Arden of Faversham* is brought to life in the courtyard of Arden's House. Abbey Street is probably the finest medieval street in the South East, but a short saunter through any of the old streets of Faversham is enough to persuade the traveller that he is in a town where history is alive at every turn. Its many claims to fame are lovingly recorded by The Faversham Society, whose members voluntarily run the splendid Fleur de Lis Heritage Centre in Preston Street, where their powers of research and organisation keep interest in the town's past bubbling and alive.

It has, they will tell you, the oldest Cinque Ports charter. The vast parish church is further proof of the town's importance in medieval times. Faversham Abbey, its stones eventually removed to reinforce the defences of English-held Calais, was bigger than Rochester or Gloucester cathedrals. The retail market, the oldest surviving in Kent, goes back more than 900 years and is held, as it has been for more than 400 years, under and around the Guildhall. And local pride is fierce. They say their apples are the best in the world. The British hop industry may be threatened by countless cases of imported lagers, but Britain's oldest surviving brewery, Shepherd Neame, in Court Street, still flourishes in private family ownership, having been in existence since 1688.

Oare – small boats and birds

Faversham, lying alongside a navigable creek, was once the largest wool-exporting port in the land and 200 years later the creek was improved to cope with all the great sailing barges loading local bricks for London. Branching off from the creek is Oare, running down to the Swale marshes, once the southern side of the old Harty Ferry, now host to small sailing boats and the occasional hopeful heron or kingfisher.

Faversham – history alive at every turn

ONE OF THE LONELY PLACES OF KENT

O let them be left, wildness and wet;
Long live the weeds and the wilderness yet.

Gerard Manley Hopkins

The remote, eastern end of the Isle of Sheppey, caravan country in summer, is silent and bleak in winter, save for the low babble of birds. The road along the ridge from Leysdown to Queenborough overlooks this lonely, marshy country, which includes Sheppey's other little islands of Elmley and Harty, where the medieval church at Sayes Court and the old Ferry House inn survive, but not the Harty Ferry. What was a short journey across the water to Oare and Faversham is now an hour's drive by car and a good two-hour return trek for the walker.

In winter, this wet grassland at Elmley Marshes, part of the extensive North Kent Marshes, attracts thousands of ducks, geese and wading birds as well as hen harriers, merlins, peregrines and short-eared owls. In summer, the avocet is among the wading birds that breed on the RSPB reserve here. There are several hides overlooking the fleets and the Swale. In August it may be possible to see more than 20 species of wader in a day at Elmley, which is also home to a range of plants of saltmarsh and rough grazing areas, as well as many species of dragonfly and damselfly.

Eastchurch, the only village on this side of the ridge, became the temporary home of some of the great pioneers of aviation: the holder of Pilots Licence No. 1, Lord Brabazon of Tara, was taught to fly on the old Eastchurch Aerodrome (now the site of an open prison), as was Sir Winston Churchill. In the 15th-century parish church, a stained-glass window commemorates two more pioneers, C. S. Rolls and Cecil Grace, who died in flying accidents in 1910. A stone memorial to the early aviators stands opposite the church.

Memorial window to aviators C. S. Rolls and Cecil Grace in Eastchurch

Elmley Marshes

Along the Medway and the Thames

From Rochester that night I went to Gravesend which is all by the side of Cherry grounds that are of several acres of ground and runs quite down to the Thames.

Celia Fiennes, 17th-century traveller

Bishop Gundulf (1024–1108) built both cathedral and castle beside the Medway at Rochester, although the castle keep on its mound, towering over the cathedral, was added in 1130. You need to go in and climb up to appreciate the great structure: four floors, walls 12 ft thick and 70 ft square and rising to 125 ft at the top of the towers, making it the tallest castle keep in England. The banqueting hall occupied the third and fourth storeys. The stunning views up and downstream from the battlements show how well it would have protected the river.

Gravesend waterfront

There is little of Gundulf's work left in the cathedral, which stands on the site of a church built in 604 AD for Justus, one of Augustine's monks and the first bishop here. It may be one of our smallest cathedrals, but there is a great deal to enjoy: those traces of Gundulf in a lovely Romanesque west front, a fine Norman nave, and a marvellous crypt; scores of fascinating reminders of the passing centuries in fabulous carved heads, wall paintings, tombs, effigies, screens; and lovely craftsmanship everywhere in wood, stone and iron.

Keep and cathedral are a fine sight from just across the river or through the windows of an approaching train as it snakes its way above the river from London to the Medway towns. In the early 18th century passengers from London, bound for the Medway towns took the 'long ferry' to Gravesend, where they were met by omnibuses. The sail boats were replaced by steam ships in the 19th century, then the coming of the railway inevitably ended the long ferry service which had begun back in the 13th century. Today, the river scene remains busy if less lively and colourful, and tourists come to Gravesend to see the resting place of the Red Indian princess Pocohontas, brought ashore here when taken fatally ill on the voyage back to Virginia.

Cathedral and castle keep, Rochester

TRAILS ACROSS THE NORTH DOWNS

This is what the people of Kent call The Garden of Eden. It is a district of meadows, cornfields, hop-gardens, and orchards of apples, pears, cherries and filberts ... At the foot of the hill ... is the village of Hollingbourne.

William Cobbett, *Rural Rides*

The chalk escarpment of the North Downs sweeps across Kent from Westerham down to Dover. Neolithic man settled the North Downs and the Medway valley more than 4,000 years ago and there are burial chambers like Kits Coty and countless finds of stone farming implements to prove it. Medieval pilgrims trudged their way to Canterbury over these Downs along the Pilgrims' Way, which frequently merges with the North Downs Way.

The North Downs are pictured here above Hollingbourne, a village which would have been a welcome resting place for those weary pilgrims, its monks offering food, drink and rest. There is plenty of real ale available here today and when the snow has gone the modern walker can set off past the Pilgrims' Way, climbing the North Downs Way on up to the steep slope of the Downs themselves. The walk becomes something of a challenge as it goes on, but the effort is eventually rewarded with wonderful views across Hollingbourne to Leeds Castle and the Greensand Ridge beyond.

Leeds Castle makes a memorable sight from any viewpoint and range. This enchanting medieval castle is built on two small islands, in the middle of a lake surrounded by 500 acres of lush green parkland. For all the restoration work in the last two centuries, what you see before you is essentially the same royal castle that Edward I bestowed on Eleanor of Castile 700 years ago. Other medieval queens who loved it as much as she did included Philippa of Hainhault, wife of Edward III, Catherine de Valois, Henry V's wife, and Catherine of Aragon, first wife of Henry VIII.

Leeds Castle – the loveliest castle in the world?

North Downs above Hollingbourne

ARCHBISHOP'S PALACE BY THE RIVER

Religion either makes men wise and virtuous, or it makes them set up false pretence to both ... Religion is, in grosser minds, an enemy to self-knowledge.

William Hazlitt, born Maidstone, 1778

This magnificent collection of medieval buildings beside the river in the heart of Maidstone is the finest sight in the county town. The Archbishop's Palace looks particularly splendid from the river. The oldest of the group, dating back to 1350 when Archbishop Islip built it with stone from his manor house in Wrotham, it was the home of the Archbishops of Canterbury until the reign of Henry VIII. Behind the church a gateway leads to what is left of the old college; the master's house is now the home of Kent Music School. A flight of stairs leads down from the gardens to the River Len, which joins the Medway here.

Completing the splendid group of riverside buildings is Archbishop Courtenay's parish church of All Saints. The Chancel was shaped to accommodate the 24 priests attached to the College. In the choir stalls are their wonderfully carved misericord seats with faces on the arm rests.

The river walk here offers welcome relief from the roar of the traffic in the one-way system above. The much-restored 13th-century bridge, across the Len on one side and the Medway on the other, bears its burdens stoically; the early stonework can be seen from the gardens below. The old palace stables house a carriage museum.

Maidstone has often been accused of shamefully spoiling and neglecting the potential beauty of its river front, but, aided by National Lottery funds, the town is establishing an £8 million Maidstone Millennium River Park. The 10 kilometre walk skirts the River Medway from Teston Country Park through Maidstone town centre to Allington and the Museum of Kent Life at Cobtree, adding new bridges where necessary, with the aim of turning the banks into a country park with free access for everyone.

Queen Victoria celebrates Christmas in the middle of Maidstone

Archbishop's Palace on the river-front

Trottiscliffe and the Distant Past

'Kent, Sir – everybody knows Kent – apples, cherries, hops and women.'

Charles Dickens, *The Pickwick Papers*

Mr Jingle has to be allowed his lyrical summary of the county at some stage and why not in this corner of Trottiscliffe – pronounced Trosley – where blossom happily meets oast? Truth to tell, the apples, cherries and hops have taken a fearful pounding from cheap foreign imports and many hop gardens and orchards have been put to the plough. Most Kentish oast houses, where hops were dried spread on the wooden floors with fires below and hot air and steam escaping through the distinctive white cowl on top, have been converted into des. res. dreams with round rooms, but they still look lovely.

This has long been farming country. In Trottiscliffe church, which stands within a group of traditional old farm buildings, away from the more modern development, are exhibits of finds from the nearby Coldrum Stones, a Neolithic burial chamber comprising a large chalk mound ringed with great stones, the biggest 12 ft by 10 ft, and trees. The finds include some of the remains of 22 people, an ox, cat, deer, rabbit and fox, all discovered when the site was excavated by the archaeologist Benjamin Harrison of Ightham, in whose memory there is a plaque on one of the stones.

The Coldrum Stones – neolithic burial chamber

One way of approaching the Coldrum Stones is through Trottiscliffe Country Park, bought in 1973 by Kent County Council. This Site of Special Scientific Interest is rich in flora and fauna, and offers families 160 acres of woods and downland with fine views across the Weald. There are short strolls and nature trails or longer walks across the Downs. Bluebells abound in spring and as the picture shows, the bright yellow of rape has now been added to the palette of Kentish countryside colours – not to everyone's delight, the heady scent clogging the senses on a hot, damp day.

Converted oast house, Trottiscliffe

THE ESSENCE OF KENT

'... this is one of the prettiest and most desirable places of residence I ever met with,' Mr Pickwick on reaching Cobham.

Charles Dickens, *The Pickwick Papers*

The brasses before the altar rail in Cobham church

Fork left in Trottiscliffe, then bear left, and you pass through Ryarsh and Birling until you can turn left again to climb up a lane cut deep in the chalk to the summit of Birling Hill, the centre of all this fine north-west Kent walking country and a glorious viewpoint. At Holly Hill there is a chance to look back again over the cement works and industrial stacks below in the Medway gap and over to the far side – where the Greensand Ridge occasionally parts to offer distant glimpses of the Wealden hills. From here you can descend past Dode, where only the church survives of the village deserted after the Black Death plague, to Luddesdown. Here a restored Norman church, a manor house and a few cottages nestle in the downs.

The manor house, Luddesdown Court, stands on the site of an early Iron Age wattle and daub dwelling. Norman, medieval and Tudor craftsmen have all left their proud marks on what has been claimed to be the oldest house in continuous occupation in England.

As you leave Luddesdown, passing under the railway, you get a glimpse of the wonderfully elegant Cobham Hall, now a girls' school. The Tudor wings were added by William Brooke, the 10th Lord Cobham, whose son narrowly escaped execution for treachery against James I – who took the house and passed it to the Duke of Lennox. It was later inherited by the Earls of Darnley, who made some glorious additions in the 18th and early 19th centuries.

Cobham has the Leather Bottle of *Pickwick Papers* fame and a church positively paved with brasses commemorating the early lords and ladies of Cobham, lying before the altar rails.

Luddesdown – quiet and lovely

Meeting Modern Demands

The 2,872 metre road crossing comprises an 812 metre cable stayed bridge with a 450 metre main span and approach viaducts of 1,052 metres on the Essex side and 1,008 metres on the Kent side.

Queen Elizabeth II Bridge website

The Queen Elizabeth II Bridge carries four lanes of M25 motorway traffic southbound across the River Thames, between Thurrock in Essex and Dartford. Two tunnels carry four lanes of traffic northbound. Work began on the bridge in August 1988 and it was officially opened by the Queen in October 1991, since when traffic has grown by 75 per cent. More than 50 million vehicles now cross each year.

A control overlooking the toll plazas on the Kent side monitors and supervises a sophisticated array of equipment to ensure the safe and efficient flow of traffic. CCTV cameras provide a continuous view of traffic conditions on both approach roads, in the tunnels and on the bridge. Sensors buried within the road deck of the bridge measure surface and air temperatures; anemometers at mid-span and on the pylons measure wind speed and direction. Lighting on the bridge had to be designed with aircraft and shipping in mind, so aircraft warning lights are located on the pylons, along with navigation lights and radar.

Bluewater – Europe's largest shopping centre

Bluewater, five miles from Gravesend, is the largest shopping centre in Europe. It opened in March 1999, receives around 80,000 visitors a day, and has 12,000 parking spaces. The 240-acres site has more than 320 stores in three malls surrounded by seven lakes, woodland and water gardens. There are also cycle paths, a boating lake and picnic areas. The effect of all this on shopping habits in the towns of Kent can only be imagined, but the lure of single-site shopping is a powerful one, particularly at Christmas.

The Queen Elizabeth II Bridge carries nearly a million vehicles per week

SHOREHAM AND THE DARENT VALLEY

And I made a rural pen,
And I stain'd the water clear,
And I wrote my happy songs
Every child may joy to hear.

William Blake, *Songs of Innocence, introduction*

Splendid views of the still remarkably remote village of Shoreham, nestling in the lovely Darent valley, can be enjoyed from benches along the waymarked footpaths on the wooded side of the valley. The village itself sits astride the River Darent, and a riverside stroll from the little bridge where the bubbling water splashes its way here and there through the village soon reveals the white house that was the home from 1827 to 1833 of Samuel Palmer, artist and etcher. Palmer's intense, mystical, pastoral landscapes reflected his devout admiration for William Blake and made this valley much loved by painters.

Bridge over the Darent, Shoreham

The artist friends coming to visit Palmer here called themselves the 'Ancients', because of their shared admiration for Early Renaissance art and their belief in the superiority of ancient over modern humanity. Blake visited him, too. The valley continued to draw the affection of artists and, a century later, another painter and talented etcher, Rowland Hilder, whose popular prints of Kent seemed for a time to hang in every living room in the land, also came to live in the valley. He, in turn, with his friends, made the valley just as familiar to another generation.

The village is well endowed with pubs and one of them, the King's Arms, has an ostler's box where the ostler waited while looking after customers' horses. The church, at the eastern end of the village, has a fine medieval carved oak rood screen and a painting commemorating Verney Lovett Cameron, son of a Victorian rector of Shoreham, who went out to Africa to find Livingstone after Stanley had left him. The great man was already dead, but Cameron and his men went on to complete the first crossing of the continent from sea to sea. Cameron later returned home here to be greeted in triumph, a day of rare clamour in a village which returned immediately to its blessed peace, save for the happy bubbling of the Darent.

Shoreham – nestling in the Darent Valley

HOME OF AN ENGLISH HERO

A day away from Chartwell is a day wasted.

Winston Churchill

Winston Churchill bought Chartwell in 1922 and made it his home for more than 40 years, enchanted by its setting in the valley enclosed by Crockham Hill and Toys Hill to the east and west, and with fine views of the Weald of Kent to the south. The house took its name from a lake in the valley, fed by the Chart Well.

The house itself being on the gloomy side of Victorian, Churchill added his 'promontory', a wing which contains three of the largest and most attractive rooms. Churchill, the painter, wanted the windows to be as large as possible so each room has them on three sides, giving a light and spacious feel and allowing those same grand views south over the garden and the Weald.

For the tourists the study, the papers, the books, the cigars, the siren suits, the walking sticks, the hats all play their part in presenting the picture of the great man. But, however well the National Trust presents the museum rooms in the house, it is in the gardens which he loved so much that his spirit seems strongest. Here he sat and ruminated, fed his golden orfe, the black swans and his ducks; here he became a bricklayer and built a really quite magnificent wall, enjoyed the blooms in the rose garden, planted trees in the orchard, and worked in his garden studio, where many of his paintings are still on display. One, unfinished, still stands on the easel.

'I think it is very important to have animals, flowers and plants in one's life while it last,' he said. His life lasted a very long time and as it retreats into history his gardens live on for visitors. In the nearby village of Westerham, Oscar Nemon's bronze statue shows him, clear eyed and belligerent of jaw. He shares the green with James Wolfe, sword drawn in war; two English heroes who carried the day.

Winston Churchill on the green at Westerham

Chartwell – the spirit lives on

TUDOR TREASURES IN CHIDDINGSTONE

God hath his soul, this town his fame
The poor a portion large of all his wordly store.

Inscription in Chiddingstone church to Richard Streatfeild

The ramparts of Chiddingstone Castle look mistily romantic early on a spring morning across the fishing lake, but this is actually a family mansion, built on the site of a medieval manor, for centuries home of the Streatfeild family. In the late 18th century Henry Streatfeild started to rebuild it in Gothic castle style, adding towers and turrets, arched windows, and even a great hall; his son continued his work in the following century.

During the 1930s the 3,000 acre estate was sold off, and from then on the castle suffered from lack of maintenance and general neglect. It was occupied by the Army during World War II and later became a school. In 1955 Denys Eyre Bower, a collector of antiques, bought the castle, and decided to display his fine Oriental and Jacobite collections there, but the great local treasure lies in the village itself.

The High Street – or at least the half that remains – is a row of perfect half-timbered 16th-century houses facing the church, built of local sandstone, the whole scene an instant step back into Tudor times. Overhanging first storeys and heavy beams, pargeting and bargeboards … no wonder film directors have found it irresistible. The National Trust, having refused to take the castle, owns and protects these handsome houses, once the homes of successful tradesmen.

The name of the Streatfeild family is prominent everywhere in the handsome church. Down a nearby footpath is the Chiding Stone, an enormous, well-worn lump of sandstone which is supposed to have given the village its name. Scolds were allegedly brought here to learn the error of their gossiping ways, although sterner sources say it means the home of the followers of a Saxon chieftain, Chid.

'… a row of perfect half-timbered 16th-century houses'

Chiddingstone Castle across the lake

OCTAVIA HILL AND THE SUMMIT OF KENT

'There needs, and will need for some time, a reformatory work which will demand that loving zeal of individuals which cannot be had for money, and cannot be legislated for by Parliament.'

Octavia Hill

Octavia Hill's grave

Toys Hill, more than 700 ft up on the Greensand Ridge above Brasted, is one of several National Trust sites of mixed woodland here offering breathtaking prospects. Emmetts, the four-acre, informal garden on neighbouring Ide Hill, was thickly screened by trees until the great storm of 1987 felled great oaks and beeches that had crowned the hill, opening up wonderful views from the car park over the Weald as far as the North Downs to the north and Crowborough Beacon to the south.

This entire lofty wooded area, which offers steep but glorious walks and is sometimes called the summit of Kent, is particularly significant to the Trust as Octavia Hill, the philanthropist and housing and educational reformer, who is buried in nearby Crockham Hill churchyard, played a leading part in the formation of the National Trust in 1895.

At the turn of the century she sunk a 100 ft well on Toys Hill to provide a local water supply for the villagers, who hauled up the bucket in pairs until it was pumped electrically. Her life was spent helping others. As a young teacher, she had been appalled at the conditions in which most of her pupils lived. She borrowed money and bought slum properties, not dispensing charity, but making sure the housing was managed properly for families.

She also believed that open spaces should be saved to be enjoyed by everyone, which ultimately led to her becoming one of the founders of the Trust. The place where she now lies offers appropriately breathtaking views, as does the well on Toys Hill, which is itself a reminder of the practical help she gave to others.

The well on Toys Hill

Colour and Creative Delight

And when your back stops aching and your hands begin to harden,
You will find yourself a partner in the Glory of the Garden.

Rudyard Kipling, *The Glory of the Garden*

Kent is wonderfully rich in gardens, not only the fine, formal grounds round the homes of the allegedly great and good and the historic properties in the care of the National Trust, but also smaller, less formal gardens that have been the inspiration and life's work of Kent families, in some cases over decades, in others over centuries.

Riverhill House, about two miles out of Sevenoaks on the main Tonbridge road, was built in 1714. In 1840 the estate became the home of the Rogers family, who still own it. This small country house is surrounded by a beautiful hillside garden dominated by great cedars of Lebanon, with fine views over the surrounding countryside.

Many of the rare trees and shrubs were planted over 150 years ago by John Rogers. There are rhododendrons and azaleas in a woodland setting and in the spring these shrubs, underplanted with bulbs, blaze like fire, as does their foliage in the autumn. There are sheltered terraces and a rose walk, which provides summer colour. An ancient trackway known as Harold's Road passes through the estate.

Great Comp Garden in Platt, near Borough Green, Sevenoaks, is an outstanding garden of about seven acres created by Eric and Joy Cameron around a 17th-century manor. Paths meander through woodland settings, then open on to wide lawns. There are formal areas and an Italian garden surrounded by walls and arches which give shelter to the more tender perennials. Other attractions include a herbaceous border, heather beds and countless informal, delightful surprises.

Informal delights at Great Comp

Rhododendrons at Riverhill

THE SPIRIT OF ROMANCE

Two thousand Deere in wildest woods I have,
Them can I take, but you I cannot hold:
He is not poore who can his freedome saue,
Bound but to you no wealth but you I would:
But take this Beast, if beasts you feare to misse,
For of his beasts the greatest beast he is

Sir Philip Sidney, *The Lady of May*, from *Songs from Arcadia*, which were inspired by the countryside around Penshurst.

The village of Penshurst lies in a narrow valley a short drive from both Tonbridge and Tunbridge Wells. Penshurst Place, reached through a walled garden, was built in 1341 by Sir John de Pulteney, four times Lord Mayor of London, who left us the magnificent Great Hall. In 1552 Henry VIII dined here in great splendour as guest of the Duke of Buckingham, the Crown acquiring the house in forfeit when the Duke was executed for treason two years later! Edward VI gave Penshurst to his steward, Sir William Sidney, father of Sir Henry Sidney. Henry started the family's work on Penshurst, which was carried on in turn by his son Philip. Sir Philip Sidney, poet, scholar, courtier, soldier, was buried with a state funeral on his gallant death in battle at the age of 31. He remains the personification of Renaissance man and the abiding spirit of Penshurst Place and its gardens.

Scotney Castle gardens – romance, colour and beauty

Penhurst Place grew into a grand stately home through many different architectural periods. The rooms reflect centuries of civilised living. The formal garden was made by Sir Henry, but much of the beauty one sees here today follows the 19th-century restoration work of an ancestor, the 2nd Lord De L'Isle. Yew hedges divide the garden and orchards into a series of delightful, self-contained garden rooms which the 1st Viscount De L'Isle rescued from years of neglect during World War II. Today, they offer glorious, ever-changing vistas of colour and form through the year.

Another of the most romantic garden settings in Kent is that of Scotney Castle, just past Lamberhurst on the A21 to Hastings. The famous 14th-century round tower, so often photographed and painted with its still reflection in the moat, and the artfully ravished ruins of the old 17th-century house make the focal point of the lovely vista created in the 19th century by the Hussey family. Their house lies at the top of the gardens, which are now in the care of the National Trust.

The fragrant rose gardens at Penshurst Place

THE SEAT OF THE SACKVILLES

The wrathful winter, 'proaching on apace,
With blustering blasts had all ybar'd the treen,
And old Saturnus, with his frosty face,
With chilling cold had pierc'd the tender green;

Thomas Sackville, 1st Earl of Dorset, who lived at Knole from 1566 to 1608.
The Mirror for Magistrates: The Induction

Knole's beautiful 1,000 acre deer park, where herds of fallow deer graze, is planted with oaks, chestnuts and beeches. Many ancient trees were lost in the great storm of 1987 and extensive replanting was necessary; but the park, extending back almost to the main street of Sevenoaks, still provides a wonderful setting for one of the finest houses in England.

Knole was the home of successive Archbishops of Canterbury until Cranmer felt obliged to give it to Henry VIII. Queen Elizabeth I bestowed it upon her Steward and Treasurer, Sir Thomas Sackville, who extended it to the essential shape we see today. His ancestors and other great figures embraced by the family over the centuries have added and embellished, to create an extraordinary array of magnificent staterooms, galleries of treasures and fine paintings, stunning furnishings, tapestries, plasterwork, and staircases, while at the same time providing a sense of continuity and a sort of lofty domesticity which constantly reassures the visitor that through all those years this has above all been a family home, however grand.

Even after a long, slow tour of the galleries and corridors and staterooms, the visitor who emerges blinking back into the 21st century and the light of the grounds outside, looks back in astonishment at the sheer size of Knole, which is alleged to represent time in days, weeks and years with seven courtyards, 52 staircases and 365 rooms. And the farther one retreats across the lovely deer park, the more remarkable it all seems: such a sea of gables, roofs, towers, turrets, battlements, chimneys can surely not be one single house?

Knole in 'the wrathful winter'

Knole Park, in the care of the National Trust

CRICKET AT TONBRIDGE SCHOOL

Reputed to be the youngest player to appear in a match at Lord's, 13-year-old Michael Cowdrey, in his first match for Tonbridge, contributed largely to the success of his side.

Wisden Cricketers' Almanack, 1947

The cricket world soon knew Michael Colin Cowdrey – the initials, of course, were MCC – by his second and third names. He played for Tonbridge 1st XI for five years, a unique achievement in English schools cricket, becoming the youngest player to be capped by Kent and going from Tonbridge up to Oxford, where he captained the University in his final year. He then played for England on the 1954–55 tour of Australia during which he made a fine century and helped to retain the Ashes. A full 20 years later he was summoned to rally the cause against blistering fast bowling on the 1974–75 tour of Australia. Cowdrey played in more than 100 Tests and scored more than 100 first class centuries. His sons Graham and Christopher played for Kent; Christopher captained England, too. And it all started on these playing fields.

Spring scene near Tonbridge

The home of Kent cricket is the St Lawrence Ground in Canterbury, where the Cricket Week is still one of the great events in the county calendar. But Tonbridge has seen many fine cricketers. E. W. Swanton once recalled: 'It was the Tonbridge nursery which produced the great professionals, Woolley, Blythe, Fielder, Freeman and others who were the backbone of Kent's first golden period, followed many years later by a second, the chief architects of which were Cowdrey and Leslie Ames.'

Cricket at Tonbridge School – the fine chapel was gutted by fire in 1988 but has been sympathetically restored.

A Place to Plight Your Troth

It is a revered thing to see an ancient castle or building not in decay.

Francis Bacon, *Of Nobility*

The great 13th-century gatehouse of Tonbridge Castle stands in pleasant gardens beside the Medway in the heart of the town. Normans and Saxons realised that the site controlled an important crossing of the river and the original, steep and massive Norman motte also survives here. In its medieval life, when it was owned by rebellious barons, the castle was besieged on a number of occasions. The gatehouse, one of the finest in England, was an impressive defence work with drawbridge, two portcullises and double doors. Edward I stayed here in 1272, 12 years after the gatehouse was built, and 250 years later the castle was described in a survey as one of the strongest in England. The Parliamentarians made the fortifications useless during the Civil War.

Today, the running water, the many trees and the extensive playing fields make this the most attractive end of Tonbridge, with some fine old houses and inns, the parish church and Tonbridge School. The oldest house in the town is Port Reeve House in East Street, which dates back more than 450 years. The Gothic mansion beside the gatehouse was built by Thomas Hooker in the 1790s, and now houses local government offices. It gives the area a more peaceful aspect, although exhibition areas in the tower feature vignettes of life in the castle and occasional martial re-enactments are still staged here.

For the most part, however, visitors admire the trees, the flowers, the river and band concerts on summer days. The castle itself has also found a more tranquil use – it is in great demand as a licensed venue for wedding ceremonies.

Bowmen take to the battlements again

The gatehouse, Tonbridge Castle

Down by the River

On the green they watch'd their sons
Playing till too dark to see,
As their fathers watch'd them once,
As my father once watch'd me;
While the bat and beetle flew
On the warm air webb'd with dew.

Edmund Blunden, who grew up in Yalding, *Forefathers*

The Beul and the Teise join the Medway at Yalding. A large field serves as a summer car park near this stretch of river bank and it is packed on July and August weekends in warm weather. The peaceful stretch pictured is all patient anglers, ramblers, picnickers and inquisitive dogs on a sunny Saturday afternoon; however, there are weirs and a lock to be treated with care a hundred yards away. On lazy midsummer weekends children splash in the shallow rapids, but the water can rise with alarming rapidity. Edmund Blunden's father was a schoolmaster here and the 'deep-dooming flood and foaming flocks of whirlwaves' of which Blunden wrote in *To Teise, a Stream in Kent* were all too clearly seen again one wild, wet autumn in the year 2000, when Yalding became nationally famous for the heavy flooding it endured.

The rivers are crossed by Yalding Town Bridge, which has been there since the 15th century, and Twyford Bridge, which is generally regarded as one of Kent's finest medieval stone bridges. Those who turn away from the river bank and explore the village will find some handsome houses, timbered, weatherboarded and of Georgian red brick, as well as fine oasts and a most unusual but attractive church tower with a blue onion dome. A more recent addition has been Yalding Organic Gardens, where a series of walks offers the visitor a tour through garden history and organic gardening techniques set against a backdrop of beautiful, mixed borders.

Riverbank, Yalding

Between Yalding and villages like Hunton and West Farleigh is hop and fruit country, with orchards and hop gardens stretching for miles.

Cherry orchard, West Farleigh

HORSMONDEN TO TUNBRIDGE WELLS

Some drink, more do not, and few drink physically; but company and diversion is in short the main diversion of the place.

Daniel Defoe on Tunbridge Wells,
Tour Thro the whole Island of Great Britain, 1724

The stretch of road from Yalding to Horsmonden is still mostly orchards and hops. A good deal of housing development has taken place in Horsmonden, but the area around the green, or heath, is attractive, having some handsome houses on the outskirts. The village expanded around a fine furnace pond and iron forge, leaving the 15th-century parish church almost alone beyond a couple of miles of serene parkland, in the direction of Goudhurst. The simple sandstone tower, surrounded by hops, crops and orchards, is a lovely, golden sight on a summer day. In the churchyard are some grand old trees and a surviving set of mounting steps, where, over the centuries, riders have climbed stiffly down before going inside to worship. This spot affords a charming view, reminiscent of a French landscape, towards Goudhurst village with its own church perched high on a hill.

Those heading back through Horsmonden towards Tunbridge Wells can encounter startlingly large juggernauts loaded with fruit, for the village is a centre for apple-growers for miles around. No traffic, though, in the Pantiles in Tunbridge Wells. Isolated in the bottom end of the town, it can hardly compete for custom with the modern shopping malls up the hill, but there can be no doubt as to which is the most classically elegant shopping parade in the town. Bath House, Musick Gallery and bandstand remain and have their day on special occasions when all manner of Georgian festivities take place. Meanwhile, all summer long, tourists and schoolchildren are served cups of allegedly invigorating water from the Chalybeate Spring, the discovery of which in 1606 eventually brought the town fame as a royal spa. For the rest of the year, friends can eat and drink here in these colonnaded walks of coffee houses and taverns while reflecting and arguing like Beau Nash and his friends in their heyday.

The Pantiles, Tunbridge Wells

Horsmonden parish church

PASSING THROUGH IN THE SPRING

... these sweet-springing meads and bursting boughs of May.

Robert Bridges, *Nightingales*

Pembury and Lamberhurst both lie on the A21 heading out of Tunbridge Wells towards Hastings and the south coast. Pembury enjoys the peace afforded by a bypass, while Lamberhurst is waiting for the same relief.

The approach to Lamberhurst is all too often seen from a lumbering line of vehicles, but it still looks attractive as traffic dips down to cross the Teise then stretches away past tiled and timbered houses up towards the other side of the valley, which is generally lush and green, particularly when lined with vines. Much of the village lies off to the right, towards Wadhurst or to Bayham Abbey ruins, and escapes the worst of the noise. The inns on either side of the river are said to have enjoyed good trade in past centuries when the river flooded and made the road impassable, a situation which recent wet seasons have made familiar again.

Lamberhurst, like Horsmonden, a few miles away down an attractive back road, had a flourishing iron foundry where iron railings were created to surround St Paul's Cathedral. The village's own 14th and 15th-century church, sitting high in an attractive setting, has a stained-glass window by John Piper and a chapel commemorating the Hussey family of Scotney Castle, whose lovely parkland lies just ahead here. There are attractive walks out from the back of the village car park, across the golf course and towards the Scotney estate.

Pembury schoolchildren dance round the maypole

Lamberhurst in the spring

BEAUTY IN MATFIELD AND BRENCHLEY

Four ducks on a pond,
A grass bank beyond,
A blue sky on spring
White clouds on the wing:
What a little thing
To remember for years
To remember with tears!

William Allingham, *A Memory*

Hop-picking near Brenchley

Turn left off the busy A21 from Pembury to Lamberhurst and you come to Matfield, where the beauty of this scene around the pond is matched only by that on the wide green beside it in the heart of the cricket season. Cream flannels still prevail here, whatever pyjamas are worn in the county one-day game, and cricketers and ducks, a hopeful young angler, elegant Matfield House and some delightful cottages on every side all contribute to the perfection of the outlook. Light traffic scurries past from Paddock Wood, heading for the bypass, but here there is no need to hurry. Passers by with dogs pause to watch an over or two, painters and photographers pause longer and a ten-minute walk with the pram can become an hour and a half on a seat, to be recalled years after one has moved house and gone.

Matfield winds down lanes on either side of a nearby crossroads, merging gradually into Brenchley, which is a village extraordinarily rich in handsome, old houses. Its pond has long gone, but the confined space round which the village stands offers wonderful timbered houses and a fine church at the end of a double row of heavily clipped yew trees. Coming out of the church, airy and light with a fine carved screen, you can climb up to the hill beyond for a magnificent view of the North Downs. The villagers chose this viewpoint for their Millennium project, providing a small fenced area, a seat and a beacon, and they chose well.

All around Brenchley lie more orchards and hop gardens from where the hops eventually find their way down to the English Hops depot in Paddock Wood below.

Village pond, Matfield

A Wealden Landscape

...and what, then, was this great church built for, if there were no more people, in those days, at Goudhurst, than there are now?

William Cobbett, *Rural Rides*

The church at Goudhurst could hardly have escaped the minds of those who laboured in the nearby orchards, fields and hop gardens, for it is visible for miles around on its high hilltop perch. When the tower is open, wonderful views can be had of this orchard and oast studded landscape. The church has many tablets and brasses in memory of the Culpeppers of Bedgebury, Tudor ironmasters, who were among the most powerful families in the Weald. From the largely 14th-century church down to the lovely pond runs a splendid descending line of Kentish pegtiled and weatherboarded houses, often at eccentric angles to the street. Other fine houses can be found around the village, testimony to its former wealth as a cloth-making centre.

The Star and Eagle inn at the top end of the village is of a similar age to the church. Indeed, the two were connected by tunnels, for this was a smugglers' pub and the notorious Hawkhurst Gang fought their last bloody gun battle with the local militia here by the church, both sides led by Goudhurst men.

A left turn after the descent to the pond heads south to Bedgebury, once the domain of the Culpeppers, but now commanded by high fir trees, for its arboretum includes the National Conifer Collection, comprising more than 1,500 varieties of conifer trees landscaped around a series of lakes and streams, complemented by broad-leaved trees, azaleas and rhododendrons.

Bedgebury Pinetum has the finest collection of conifers in the world

Characteristic Kentish landscape near Goudhurst

CLOTH TRADE PROSPERITY

Love is like linen, often chang'd, the sweeter

Phineas Fletcher, born in Cranbrook, 1582, *Siclides*

As the weaving centre of the region from the 14th to 17th centuries, Cranbrook was one of the most important towns in the Weald. The cloth trade brought wealth and fine houses here. The weavers worked at their craft in the 16th-century Old Cloth Hall, just outside the town. Queen Elizabeth I is said to have walked to Coursehorn, half-a-mile away, on a pathway of Cranbrook broadcloth, laid down by Flemish weavers.

The white weatherboarded buildings are dominated by the white smock Union Mill, in perfect condition and still grinding flour for bread; but the church, sometimes called the Cathedral of the Weald, is also a splendid building, all bright light and generous space. It was the rich Flemish merchants who made possible many of the 15th and 16th-century additions. Nearby Cranbrook School, 'a free and perpetual grammar school' received its Royal charter from Queen Elizabeth in 1574. She stayed at the George Hotel. All over the town there are houses and pubs of handsome character, red tile-hung or white weatherboarded, brilliant in sunlight and gleaming in rain, offering delight at every turn.

There is further evidence of the flourishing local cloth trade at Biddenden, reached from Cranbrook through Sissinghurst: another Old Cloth Hall, a particularly fine one, and more beautiful half-timbered houses to be seen. The village sign on the green commemorates the two Maids of Biddenden, Siamese twins, who are said to have lived in Elizabethan times. Another memory of them lingers on in the form of a local charity in aid of the poor of the parish. This is one of the best-preserved of the Wealden villages. Claris's is the perfect place to stop for irresistible cakes and coffee, particularly in winter, when the tourists have gone.

Claris's in Biddenden – irresistible cakes

The Union Mill towers over Cranbrook

SISSINGHURST

The place, when I first saw it on a spring day in 1930, caught instantly at my heart and my imagination.

Vita Sackville-West

Sissinghurst, lying in lovely countryside between Cranbrook and Biddenden, is another attractive Wealden village with some fine old cottages. The main attraction here, however, is nearby Sissinghurst Castle and its gardens, now run by the National Trust but created by Sir Harold Nicholson and Vita Sackville-West, who came here in 1930 and turned a ruin and a wilderness into one of the best-loved gardens in the country. Against the background of the romantic Elizabethan prospect tower, they used yew and hornbeam hedges and what remained of the old brickwork, which they clad in clematis, honeysuckle and magnolia, to create a series of intimate enclosed gardens linked by lovely walks.

Harold Nicholson was the classical designer, his wife the joyous and abundant planter. Not for her serried ranks of blooms. She planted by shade and blend of colour, by texture and season. Always keeping to their original design and meticulously recording every planting, the pair created the perfect English garden. The Nuttery is all primroses and polyanthus, the Lime Walk alive with thousands of spring bulbs, the Cottage Garden a riot of red, orange and yellow against the dark green of the yew. The Rose Garden offers cascades of roses blooming in wonderfully fragrant and colourful glory in June and July, many of them old varieties saved from extinction. The Wild Garden in the orchard is a complete contrast to the famous White Garden, where lavender, roses, clematis and a double primrose are all

The roses are the greatest of Sissinghurst's glories

white or off-white and the foliage is mostly grey. Everywhere there are brilliantly designed surprise prospects and views, some of small scale features, others of distances.

A staircase leads past Vita Sackville-West's study to the top of the tower from where the view is memorable, looking out across the Weald to the distant North Downs. But to look down is to see the gardens in all their glory and they, too, once seen, are never forgotten.

Near Sissinghurst, at dawn

JEWEL OF THE WEALD

This Tenterden is a market town and an exceedingly bright spot. It consists of one street, which is, in some places, more, perhaps, than two hundred feet … The town is upon a hill …

William Cobbett, *Rural Rides*

Tenterden, standing on high land between the Rother Levels and the River Beult valley, is yet another Wealden town which found prosperity in the wool trade, enjoying not only abundant wool from the sheep on the marshes, but also access to the sea until the 16th century when the marsh ports silted up. The beautiful 15th-century pinnacled tower of the parish church, dedicated to St Mildred, Abbess of Minster, was raised largely by the efforts of Flemish wool merchants; next to the church is the Woolpack Inn from the same century.

The Town Hall, beside the inn, was built in 1792 and includes a splendidly restored Assembly Room. The church tower can be seen across the flat landscape for miles around, although in the town itself it seems to vanish, only to rise unexpectedly and peep through over the rising and falling rooftops of the wonderfully varied buildings in the High Street. There are sturdy timber-framed houses from Tudor days, elegant Georgian bow-windows and doorways, white weatherboarded houses, Victorian red hanging tiles, and yet somehow all fit perfectly together in one long street, wide with plenty of green spaces and trees at the ends.

Just off the High Street is Tenterden Town Station, terminus of the Kent and East Sussex Railway, Kent's only full-size steam railway. The registered charity has restored much of the disused Rother Valley Railway line in stages and now offers a nostalgic 10-mile run to Bodiam, with its beautiful castle, just over the Sussex border, in old carriages pulled by steam engines of widely varied pedigrees; a journey of sheer delight.

Tenterden Town Station on the Kent and East Sussex Railway

Tenterden High Street – high, wide and handsome

KEEPING BONAPARTE OFF THE MARSHES

When the late Mr Pitt was determined to keep out Bonaparte and prevent his gaining a settlement in the county of Kent, among other ingenious devices adopted for that purpose he caused to be constructed what was then, and has ever since been, conventionally a 'Military Canal' ...

Richard Barham, *The Ingoldsby Legends*

A stranger to Kent stumbling upon the Royal Military Canal on a tranquil autumn morning might at first suppose it to be a lost river. It is certainly a far cry from the narrow cuts of the commercial canal system. But it was built not to carry freight but, as Richard Barham observes, as a defence against invasion by Napoleon early in the 19th century – although he was clearly not persuaded that Bonaparte actually had designs on the route to Ashford. The canal runs from Hythe in a semicircle of more than 20 miles through the flat fields of the Romney Marsh to a point north of Rye.

Never tested as a defence work, it became a much-loved retreat for ramblers, picnickers and waterfowl. The National Trust owns the lovely stretch of the canal between Appledore, a handsome historic village with fine old houses in a wide main street, and Warehorne, where Barham lived and served as curate, as well as rector of Snargate. This part of the Marsh is known as the Dowels.

In Hythe, the canal assumes a totally different role, running through the middle of the town surrounded by tall trees and providing a pleasure boat stretch of water for casual rowers and the setting for a Venetian water carnival. William Cobbett was also contemptuous of it as a defence work, and of the

The canal on the Kent/East Sussex border

Martello towers, two of which survive on Hythe's pleasant seafront. Hythe is the terminus of the famous narrow-gauge Romney, Hythe and Dymchurch Railway, which runs for 13 miles across the marshes through Dymchurch and New Romney to Dungeness. The shrill whistle of the still beautiful little steam engines can be heard far across the marshes, by birdwatchers in the Dungeness sanctuary, or by fishermen along the seashore at Greatstone.

Royal Military Canal

THE CHURCHES OF ROMNEY MARSH

Mother of Stars! enthroned I lie
On the high bed of your kindness sent
And see between the marsh and sky
The little lovely hills of Kent.

E. Nesbit, Dymchurch, 1924

Fairlight church, dedicated to St Thomas à Becket, is a perfect expression of the spirit of Romney Marsh. It stands beside water, quite alone, reached along a grass causeway. There is no road, no churchyard, no screen of trees. Sheep graze up to the door and the insistent breezes from the distant sea, Richard Church's 'subtle wind-music in the marsh', ripple the grass around it.

The church was built in the 13th century and restored in 1913. In the distance, a few farms and outbuildings give the only clues to the identities of the congregation. Inside, there are six simple box pews, a pulpit on three levels – sermon from the top one, lessons from the next, clerk at the bottom – and an old stone font. When the marsh was flooded they came here by boat to worship.

A mile or so to the west lies St Mary in the Marsh, another remote marshland church. Backed by trees and set in fields, opposite an inn, it is partly Norman with later additions. There are some attractive carvings and brasses and a memorial tablet to E. Nesbit, one of the most loved of English children's writers. The author of *The Railway Children*, *Five Children and It*, *The Phoenix and the Carpet* and *The Wouldbegoods* came to live near Dymchurch and in her last days, her friend the actress Dame Sybil Thorndyke, arranged to have her bed raised so that she could see out across the marsh. She wrote her last words there (above) and was buried in the peaceful churchyard of St Mary in the Marsh.

St Mary in the Marsh – resting place of E. Nesbit

Fairfield Church – splendid isolation

Fresh Fish at Dungeness

'... before this Neshe lieth a flat into the Sea, threatening great danger to unadvised sailers.'

William Lambarde on Dungeness

Power stations and pylons, shanty shacks and shingle spit, anglers on the shifting shore and fishing boats out at sea, two lighthouses, lifeboat station, bird sanctuary, wicked wind off the water and fresh fish on sale for tea: Dungeness is an extraordinary jumble of images.

It is certainly desolate, particularly outside high summer; but then that is half the attraction to those lonely anglers, birdwatchers and botanists drawn to the rare plants on the shingle in this dynamic landscape, or geologists, fascinated by the greatest shingle structure in Britain. The fishermen's huts have net lofts and smokeries; the converted railway carriages are for weekenders; work and leisure; top enders and bottom enders. Before roads were laid, locals wore 'backstays' on the soles of their boots and shoes – the shingle equivalent of snowshoes.

The strange atmospheric wilderness has always attracted artists, such as Paul Nash, John Piper, Eric Ravilious – and film director Derek Jarman, who created an extraordinary little garden on the shingle in front of his famous black bungalow, with driftwood and plants from the seashore. The power stations and the pylons may be grim intruders on this unique prospect, but people will always feel its strange attractions, while they watch the fishermen or admire the fine coastal view from the top of the old lighthouse. Then they might enjoy fish and chips at The Pilot below, before riding back down the narrow gauge line of the Romney, Hythe and Dymchurch Railway, while the gulls call a raucous farewell from above the stony wilderness which is Dungeness.

Anglers on the shingle bank

Fishing boats off Dungeness

The river Rother on the Kent-East Sussex border

Kent is very much a rural county. In his evocative photographs, David Sellman seeks to reflect the country in all its moods and colours: from the golden hues of autumn, the white frosts of winter and the gentle greens of spring to the blaze of the summer sun. The text, by the former editor of *Kent Life*, Rod Cooper, chronicles the county's history and demonstrates just how much it has to offer today, both to local people and visitors alike.

David Sellman first started taking photographs at the age of ten, using a Kodak Brownie and then a Zeiss Ikonta, at that time on black and white film. On leaving school he worked in a studio in London's West End and his duties included assisting Cecil Beaton, sometimes on royal sittings. After ten years in London he moved to a firm in the Kent countryside and became a photographic colour printer producing giant photographic enlargements for film backgrounds. The outdoor life beckoned and he turned to landscape photography, first in Kent and Sussex, and then nationwide. All work is now in colour and cameras used are a Mamiya and a Wista.

Rod Cooper has edited the county magazines of Kent, Sussex and Surrey over the last twenty years and has written several books. He is now a full-time author and lives on the Kent-Sussex border.

Front cover photograph: Horsmonden
Back cover photograph: The Queen Elizabeth II Bridge